40
HADITHS

FOR CHILDREN WITH STORIES

By : Prof. Dr. M. Yasar KANDEMIR

New Edition : 2013

Kutub Khana Ishayat-ul-Islam
125A, Sant Nagar, New Delhi - 110065 (India)

CONTENTS

FOREWORD

My dear children, God Almighty wishes for all His servants to be happy. He sent us prophets in order to teach us how. The prophets are the guides and teachers of human beings. They teach us the commands of Allah Almighty and how we should live in this world. This has been so since the first prophet, Adam, to the last prophet, Muhammad (peace be upon them).

As you already know, the sayings of our Prophet are called *hadiths*. Our beloved Prophet (peace be upon him), who brought us the Qur'an or the commands of our Lord, explained to us these Divine commands through his hadith. He taught us through his sayings what we need to do in order to be happy both in this life and in the Hereafter.

We should often read the holy sayings of our Prophet if we want to understand the commands of Almighty God, and if we want to learn our religion in the most perfect way. For centuries many Muslim scholars have put our Prophet's sayings together into bouquets of forty which made them easier to learn.

I also wanted my fortieth book, which I have written for you, to be a collection of forty sayings

3

of our glorious Prophet. I know that you like very much to read stories, so I have presented these sayings in the form of tales written around the sayings of the Prophet. My beloved children, I hope you will enjoy reading this book, and if you like it, would you please pray for me?

M. Yasar Kandemir

4

THE BIRDS

One day, a hunter set his net on the banks of a stream. Many birds, which got lured by the grain in the net, fell into his trap. When the hunter came to gather his net, the birds suddenly flew away with the net.

The hunter was astonished by their cooperation and coordination when he saw all the birds flying together with the net. He decided to follow them to see what was going to happen.

A man, whom he met on his way, asked him where he was rushing to.

Pointing the birds in the sky, the hunter said he was going to catch the birds.

The man laughed and said:

"May God grant you some sense! Do you really think you can catch birds on the wing?"

The hunter said:

"If there was only one bird in the net I wouldn't stand a chance. But wait and see; I will catch them."

"The hunter was right. When the night fell, the birds all wanted to go to their own nests. Some of them pulled the net to the woods, others

headed toward the lake. Some wanted to fly to the mountains, others to the bushes. None succeeded and finally all of them crashed down with the net. The hunter came and caught all of the birds.

Poor birds! If only they had known the following saying of our Prophet they would have always flown in the same direction, and then they would not have gotten caught by the hunter:

"Do not separate from one another! The lamb that abandons its herd will be eaten by the wolf."

فَعَلَيْكُمْ بِالْجَمَاعَةِ فَإِنَّمَا
يَأْكُلُ الذِّئْبُ الْقَاصِيَة

رواه النسائي.

A THORN

Once upon a time there was a terrible punishment under way in a certain country. They were feeding the criminals to the hungry lions. People would gather to watch this horrifying scene.

The criminal that day was a slave who had escaped from his owner. He was left in the middle of an arena surrounded by high walls. They let a hungry lion into the arena. At first the lion got ready to pounce on the poor man, but suddenly it stopped and started to lick the slave's hands!

The spectators were astonished. They asked the slave why the lion had not attacked him.

The slave said:

"One day, I saw this lion in the forest. A thorn had lodged itself in its paw, and it was in great pain. I pulled out the thorn and since that day we have been good friends."

People got touched by this story. They set both the lion and the slave free. To the people's amazement the lion was following the slave as if it was his pet cat.

What a wonderful saying of our Prophet:

"God shows his mercy to those who are merciful. Have compassion to creatures on earth so that those in heaven may have mercy upon you."

الرَّاحِمُونَ يَرْحَمُهُمُ الرَّحْمَانُ، ارحموا مَنْ فِي الأَرْضِ يَرْحَمْكُمْ مَنْ فِي السَّمَاءِ

رواه الترمذي.

THE COAT

Ahmad the shepherd was very sad. He had lost almost everything he owned during the terrible years of war. His wife had died and he had also lost his son. When he lost his job in town, he began to work as a shepherd in the countryside.

One day, as his sheep grazed near the road, he saw a group of people taking a young man to the hospital in town. It was obvious that this young man was even poorer than him. He was shivering in his thin jacket. Ahmad the shepherd immediately took off his own coat, which he had owned for years, and put it on the young man.

As the young man was waiting in the hospital to be examined, he was surprised to hear someone calling him "Dad." He looked up but he couldn't recognize the young man standing in front of him. The latter, who had called him dad, was surprised as well.

He apologized, saying, "I'm sorry, sir. I had mistaken your coat for my father's, whom I haven't seen for many years. I thought you were my father."

The sick man asked him who his father was. After talking for a few minutes, he realized that the young man was the lost son of Ahmad the shepherd. He told the young man that he did not make a mistake and that the coat had really belonged to his father. After being examined at the hospital, he returned to the village, accompanied by shepherd Ahmad's son.

How true is the saying of our beloved Prophet,

"Every kindness will be rewarded tenfold."

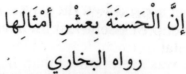

إِنَّ الْحَسَنَةَ بِعَشْرِ أَمْثَالِهَا

رواه البخاري

THE MIRROR

Once upon a time, a vizier was walking around the market with his high officials. He came across the slave market. Pitiful people who had lost their freedom were being sold one by one.

The vizier approached the slaves. He wanted to see them more closely. Just then, an old slave said to the vizier:

"There is a stain on your turban, sir."

The vizier took off his turban and examined it. The slave was right. This meant that he had been walking through the market with a stained turban for hours and everybody had seen it. How embarrassing! Then he looked at his companions sadly and said to them:

"You saw the stain on my turban, yet you closed your eyes and didn't tell me anything about it. I just realized that my real fried was that poor slave. I cannot let my true friend be sold as a slave! Buy him immediately and set him free."

Later, the vizier had the following hadith of the Prophet framed and sent it to his men so that they would never forget this incident:

"A Muslim is the mirror of another Muslim."

الْمُؤْمِنُ مِرْآةُ الْمُؤْمِنِ

رواه أبو داود

THE 'MEANIE'

*I*t was a beautiful summer day and children were playing on the shore of a stream. Among them was a boy named Gaffar, but all the children called him 'Meanie' because of his cruel treatment to animals. Gaffar was bored with the game they were playing; he wanted to play something that was more exciting and interesting. The other children made some suggestions, but he thought they were all boring.

Gaffar called aside some of his friends who thought like him. Soon they announced that they had come up with a fun game.

The other children wondered what this game could be.

Gaffar and his friends sneaked behind their friend Ali, who was new in town, and didn't know how to swim. They caught his hands and legs and threw poor Ali into the stream!

Ali panicked. He struggled hard to swim, but the harder he tried the more he sank. He started screaming for help. Gaffar and his friends were laughing as he screamed.

One of the other children quickly took off his clothes. It was Ismail. Ismail was a brave kid and only he could stand up to Gaffar. As soon as he saw what they had done to Ali, he rose up against them. In a few minutes, he brought Ali safely to shore.

The other children congratulated Ismail. A man passing by had seen everything. The well-dressed, kind-faced man went up to Ismail, and putting his hand on his shoulder, said:

"My dear boy, you have acted just as the way our beloved Prophet has ordered. May Allah be pleased with you. Our Prophet said in one of his hadiths:

"A Muslim is the brother of another Muslim.

He neither oppresses him nor leaves him in evil hands."

الْمُسْلِمُ أَخُو الْمُسْلِمِ

لاَ يَظْلِمُهُ ولاَ يُسْلِمُهُ

رواه البخاري

A GHOST

Once upon a time, a trader was coming back home late at night. Suddenly he saw an old, poor black man preparing to spend the night next to a wall. No one accepted him into their houses fearing that their children would be scared of him. The trader decided to help him. He took him into his house, offered him hot soup, gave him clean clothes and a room to stay.

In the middle of the night, the old man sleeping near the window suddenly woke up with a noise. He saw that two burglars were trying to enter the house through the window.

The black man raised his hands and shouted loudly;

"What are you doing there?"

"Oh my mother! A ghost!" screamed the burglars when they saw the black man in white pajamas, and they threw themselves from the window. One of them broke his leg and the other injured his head. Because of the noise, the trader and his family woke up and they captured the burglars.

How wonderful is the reminder of our Prophet:

"Certainly Allah helps His servant, as long as he helps his brother!"

وَاللهُ في عَوْنِ العَبدِ ما كَانَ العَبْدُ
في عَونِ أخِيهِ

رواه مسلم

17

A NEIGHBOR IN PARADISE

Once upon a time a Sultan was walking around the cities. He had changed his clothes so that no one would recognize him and he took one of his slaves with him. He wanted to know what his people really thought about his administration.

It was winter and very cold. He went into a small mosque. Two poor men were sitting in a corner, shivering. They had no place to go. The Sultan approached them, wondering what they were talking about.

The funny one was complaining about the cold weather: "After

I die, when we go to Paradise, I will not let our Sultan enter Paradise. If I see him approaching the gates, I will take off my shoe and hit him on the head." The second man asked, curiously:

"Why would you keep our Sultan out of Paradise?"

"Of course I would not let him enter. While we are freezing here, he is sitting comfortably in his warm palace; he doesn't know how we live. How can he be my neighbor in Paradise? I don't need any such neighbor there." They both laughed.

The Sultan said to his slave:

"Do not forget this small mosque and these two men."

When the Sultan returned to the palace, he sent his men to the mosque. They brought the two poor men to the palace. The two men were puzzled about what was going on. After they waited in fear, they were taken into a luxurious room and were told:

"You shall eat, drink, and live here and you shall pray for our Sultan and you shall not object for him to be your neighbor in Paradise!"

What a kind-hearted Sultan he is, isn't he?

Our Prophet (peace be upon him) praised those who help the needy in the following hadith:

"Whosoever takes care of a believer's need in this world, God will take care of his need in the Hereafter."

مَنْ نَفَّسَ عَنْ مُؤْمِنٍ كُرْبَةً مِنْ كُرَبِ الدُّنْيَا نَفَّسَ اللَّهُ عَنْهُ كُرْبَةً مِنْ كُرَبِ يَوْمِ الْقِيَامَة

رواه مسلم

TOOTH MEDICINE

One day a very well-dressed stranger went to a restaurant in town.

He told the waiter:

"I would like some well-done roast beef and some salad, please."

As soon as he bit his first piece, he screamed with pain: "Ahhhhh! My tooth is hurting again!" Another stranger approached, holding a large bag in his hand. He took a small bottle from his bag. He poured some liquid onto a piece of cotton and handed it to the man in pain.

"Swipe this cotton on your aching tooth," he said.

The man did as he was told. Suddenly, he exclaimed:

"Strange! I don't feel the pain anymore!"

Everyone gathered around the man with the large bag asking to buy that wonderful drug. The bottles in his bag were soon sold out.

An hour later, the man with the toothache and the man with the bag met at the railway station. They discussed how profitable their business had been in that town and congratulated one another. They sat and waited for the next train.

Just then two policemen came and arrested them.

One of the people who had bought the fake medicine had gone to the police station when the medicine hadn't stopped his toothache.

The police chief called the two men into his office and asked them:

"What is your religion? Are you Muslim?"

Without raising their heads, they said

"We are Muslim, thank God."

The police chief got even angrier.

"Have you not heard the hadith of our Prophet:

"Whoever deceives us is not one of us."

مَنْ غَشَّنَا فَلَيْسَ مِنَّا

رواه مسلم

Then he punished the men.

THE WALLET

Once upon a time, there was an ill-natured merchant who had lost his purse at the market with 800 gold coins in it. He looked everywhere trying to find it, and asked everyone if they had seen it, but he couldn't find it nor had anyone seen it. Then he hired a town crier to announce that he would give one hundred gold pieces as a reward to anyone who found the wallet.

A man known as Veli the Shoemaker found the lost purse. He was a very honest man. He decided to keep the purse until he could find its owner. When he heard the town crier making an announcement he went to the trader and gave the purse back.

The trader was not only ill-natured; he was also stingy and a liar. He was happy that his purse had been found, but he did not reveal this to Veli.

He opened the purse and started to count his money, saying:

"Oh! I see you have already taken the money I had promised as a reward."

Veli took hold of the merchant's lapels and shook him.

"How dare you! Yes, I am poor, but I am not a thief or a scoundrel. You don't have to give me the money you promised, but do not accuse me of stealing your money!"

When the merchant did not retract his accusation, they both ended up in court. After listening to both sides, the judge realized the merchant was lying. He decided to give him a heavy punishment.

"The merchant says that 100 gold liras were taken from his purse, yet the shoemaker says that he did not take any money. I believe both parties. I guess the purse found by the shoemaker was not the merchant's, rather it belongs to somebody else. Therefore, it will stay under protection until the real owner is found.

The miserly merchant regretted his actions, but it was too late. This reminds us one of the Prophet's hadith:

"He who doesn't thank people does not thank God either."

مَنْ لاَ يَشْكُرُ النَّاسَ لاَ يَشْكُرُ اللهُ

رواه الترمذي

THE POISON

*H*uusayin was returning from town to his village. He was happy because he had sold all his goods in the town's market. He stopped to rest by a fountain.

"I'll let my donkey graze a bit, while I have a snooze under that tree," he thought.

Just as he was about to sleep, he remembered the money in his moneybag. He thought he should put it in a safe place. He opened it and looked at the coins. They all were there, and there were none missing. He put the bag inside his shirt and drifted off to sleep.

Unfortunately, there was a thief in the tree who saw everything. The thief was a very bad man and he had spent all his life harming other people. His eyes glimmered when he saw Husayin's moneybag. Slowly, he climbed down the tree and took out a straw and a jar of poison. He spread some of the poison on the straw.

He silently approached Husayin, who was sleeping deeply. He planned to kill him and take his money by simply blowing the poison through the straw into Husayin's mouth.

Just as the thief was about to administer the poison, Huseyin suddenly sneezed.

The thief was surprised, and swallowed, taking all the poison into his mouth. He died immediately.

Our Prophet said:

"Allah harms the person who hurts others."

مَنْ ضَارَّ ضَارَّ اللهُ بِهِ

رواه الترمذي

26

THE BELT

Nihat was a very naughty child. He used to hurt his brothers. He was always quarreling and was very rude. His behavior upset his mother terribly. She would always advise him:

"Dear, don't hurt other people's feelings. Don't say rude things to people."

But Nihat would never admit that he was wrong. He would say:

"It's not my fault. I haven't done anything wrong. They made me angry, which made me behave like that."

One day his mother told him that if he didn't quarrel with anyone until evening she would buy him a belt that he had seen in a shop window. He really wanted that belt.

His brothers overheard what his mother had said and tried to pick an argument with him. But they couldn't make him angry; Nihat had decided to control himself for once.

In the evening his mother called him:

"I see that you can control yourself for a belt. You should do this for God, as this is what He ordered, not for simple, material things."

If only someone had told Nihat the following hadith:

"I guarantee that anyone who does not fight even when provoked, shall be given a mansion in paradise."

مَنْ تَرَكَ الْمِرَاءَ وَهُوَ مُحِقٌّ بُنِيَ لَهُ فِي وَسَطِ الْجَنَّةِ

رواه الترمذي

ANGER

*H*alit was a very strong child. He could lift a stool straight up from the ground with only one hand.

Nobody could beat him at school in wrestling. He mostly wrestled against his friend Nurettin.

One day Nurettin and Halit wrestled in the schoolyard again. Nurettin lost. He was so angry that he went into the classroom and scribbled all over Halit's books.

This made Halit very angry. He jumped on Nurettin and punched him on the nose.

Nurettin's nose started to bleed, and the blood got all over his clothes and on the classroom floor.

Their classmates all felt bad when they saw what had happened. The teacher scolded Halit and told him the following hadith:

"A strong person is not the one who beats his rivals in wrestling, but a strong person is the one who controls his anger."

لَيْسَ الشَّدِيدُ بِالصُّرَعَةِ إِنَّمَا الشَّدِيدُ الَّذِي يَمْلِكُ نَفْسَهُ عِنْدَ الْغَضَبِ
رواه البخاري

THE RACE

*H*usnu was a good child. Unfortunately, he had lost his sight in a traffic accident, but he never gave up on life. Every day he demonstrated that he could manage to live without being a burden to others. Many times he even went from his village to the town and came back all by himself.

In the same village there was an arrogant boy called Murtaza. One day, Murtaza wanted to make fun of Husnu and challenged him to a race from the village to the town.

Husnu accepted. "Okay, but on one condition. If I win the race, you will give me your jacket."

Murtaza laughed. "If you win, you can have the jacket," he said.

Husnu had one more condition. "I set the time for the race."

Murtaza thought that Husnu would never win, so he agreed.

Husnu set the time of the race for a moonless night.

The road to the town passed through the forest. It didn't matter to Husnu if it was night or day. He walked as he always did and reached the town. But Murtaza got lost. He fell down into many holes and branches whipped his face. He arrived in the town half an hour later than Husnu.

Poor Murtaza! If only he had known the following hadith then he wouldn't have acted in such a way.

"Allah revealed to me: 'Be humble and let none of you be arrogant toward others.'"

$$إِنَّ اللهَ عَزَّ وَجَلَّ أَوْحَى إِلَيَّ أَنْ تَوَاضَعُوا$$

$$حَتَّى لَا يَفْخَرَ أَحَدٌ عَلَى أَحَدٍ$$

رواه مسلم

THE GOLD

*A*ylin was a snobbish and arrogant girl. But then one day her father died and she became very depressed.

She always played by herself in the garden of their villa. She didn't want to talk to the girl next door, Bedriye, because they were very poor.

One day Bedriye came running into Aylin's garden, saying:

"My father is very ill. He could be dying. He wants to see you. He wants to say something very important to you."

Aylin spurned and said:

"As if a poor man can tell me something important! Your house probably smells really bad and no one would want to go into a bad-smelling house."

A few minutes later Bedriye came back with tears in her eyes.

"My father has to tell you something really important. Your father buried some gold just before he died. Only my father knows where the gold is buried.

"Your father told him not to mention the gold to you until you became a grown up, but as he is about to die he wants to tell you now. Please hurry!"

When Aylin heard what Bedriye was saying she ran to the neighbor's house. But they were too late; the poor man had just died.

Aylin was very angry with herself and she regretted her actions.

Was the gold the only thing that she had lost? No, she had also lost her chance to get to Paradise because she had clung to her old bad habits.

Our Prophet said the following for such people:

"No one who has arrogance in his/her heart shall enter paradise, even the weight of a mustard seed."

لَا يَدْخُلُ الْجَنَّةَ مَنْ كَانَ
فِي قَلْبِهِ مِثْقَالُ ذَرَّةٍ مِنْ كِبْرٍ
رواه مسلم

THE THIEF

Nuri was a poor, simple farmer. Some people thought he was an incompetent loser because he never meddled himself in anybody's business and wouldn't speak unless he had to.

One day, someone who was previously reputed to be a wise person stole Nuri's donkey. When he saw that his donkey had gone, Nuri set out to the market to buy a new donkey.

As he was walking around the market he saw his own donkey there for sale. He went up to the seller and said:

"This is my donkey. It was stolen from me last week."

The thief was a man without shame. He replied:

"You're mistaken; I bought this donkey when it was a foal and raised it myself."

When Nuri heard this, an idea occurred to him. He covered the donkey's eyes and said:

"If this is your donkey, then tell me, which is his blind eye?"

The thief hesitated a moment, and then replied:

"His right eye."

Nuri uncovered the eye and showed the seller that the eye could see just fine.

"Oh, I'm sorry, I got confused. Of course, it's his left eye."

"Once again, you are wrong," said Nuri, opening the left eye. The other people in the market had gathered around. They realized that it was really Nuri who was the wise man.

Our Prophet cursed those people who steal other people's belongings:

"May Allah Almighty curse thieves!"

لَعَنَ اللَّهُ السَّارِقَ

رواه البخاري

36

THE MORSEL

*B*esim was a good child. His father was wealthy, so he had everything he wanted. But he knew nothing about how less fortunate people lived.

One day, as he was going to play football, a dog started to chase him. He ran very fast but the dog caught him in a narrow alley. Just then, Besim stumbled over a stone and fell down.

When he opened his eyes he saw a boy, about his own age, and the boy's mother. The mother was dressing his wounds. They had saved him from the dog and took him to their home to clean his wounds.

Besim thanked them. He was very surprised when he saw their home. Their furniture was very simple and ordinary.

When he sat down to share dinner with them he was very uncomfortable. He felt that every bite he ate stuck in his throat.

The next day Besim took some food prepared by his mother to the boy and his mother. Then he ate dinner with them; this time he felt better about what he ate. Soon the two boys became good friends.

Besim was a merciful and kind child, and this is why he behaved in accordance with the following hadith of the Prophet:

"The person who is sated while his or her neighbors are hungry is not a Muslim."

مَا آمَنَ بِي مَنْ بَاتَ شَبْعَانَ وَجَارُهُ

جَائِعٌ إِلَى جَنْبِهِ وَهُوَ يَعْلَمُ بِهِ

رواه إبن أبي شيبة

THE MONEY

It was Ramadan and Ethem had gone to the bakery to buy some bread to get ready for *iftar*. There was a long queue in front of the bakery. As the time to break the fast approached the people became more and more impatient.

The baker was worried about the people in the queue. It was not easy for him to work quickly, to make sure everybody had bread and take the correct money. It was almost time to break fast when Ethem's turn came. The baker was really tired by that time, and by mistake he gave Ethem too much change. At first Ethem hesitated, and looked at the baker's face in surprise.

"Is there something wrong?" the baker asked.

"No," Ethem said and he took the money. He ran home from the bakery.

At dinner Ethem was worried and distracted. When he went to bed that night he became even more worried. He felt as if an invisible man was asking him:

"Why did you do that? Why did you take money that wasn't yours?"

He thought that he should tell his mother everything; but then he changed his mind and didn't say anything. He knew that his mother would be

angry and blame him.

He had nightmares all night long. When he woke up in the morning he didn't feel better.

He looked at the calendar on the wall. There was a hadith written there, which read as follows:

"Sin is the thing which disturbs your heart and the thing you don't want others to know."

الإِثْمُ مَا حَاكَ فِي صَدْرِكَ

وَكَرِهْتَ أَنْ يَطَّلِعَ عَلَيْهِ النَّاسُ

رواه مسلم

Ethem felt his face turning red, as if our beloved Prophet had spoken this hadith just for him. He immediately went to the bakery and gave the baker's money back, apologizing for not having returned it sooner.

THE MEDIATOR

*I*t was a cold winter day. Isa was going to school when he ran across a poor child. The child wasn't even wearing a coat. His shoes were old, worn and wet. Isa was moved when he saw this. His family wasn't rich either, but they could buy what their son needed.

Isa decided to follow this boy. He was surprised to see that the boy was going to the same school. He didn't recognize him from school; he hadn't seen him there before. He wondered what he could do to help the boy, but he didn't know what. He would have given his boots that he had been wearing for two years, but he didn't have a spare pair.

At lunchtime he saw the boy again and asked him if he wanted to be friends. Soon they became really good friends. The other boy's father had died a few years ago. He lived with his mother and

two little sisters and they had just moved to the neighborhood. Isa shared his lunch with him that day.

That evening, Isa said to his father:

"Our teacher gave us an assignment today. We need to find out how we can help the poor."

His father gave him some ideas and told him of some ways to help the poor.

The next day, Isa went to the "Help the Poor Foundation" in the neighborhood. He met a man there, who had a very kind face. He told him about his friend's situation and asked for help. The man became very happy for what Isa had done and congratulated him for his action. He told Isa to find out where his friend lived and said to him:

"Both Allah Almighty and our Prophet love children like you. You have acted in accordance with the following hadith:

"One who mediates for charity is rewarded by God as if he had performed this charity himself."

إِنَّ الدَّالَّ عَلَى الْخَيْرِ كَفَاعِلِهِ

رواه الترمذي

HIDE AND SEEK

*I*hsan was playing hide and seek with his friends. When it was time to hide he found a good hiding place behind a chestnut tree near the street. It would be hard to find him there!

Just then, an old man with a white beard came up to him. The man was a stranger.

"Son, I need directions, can you help me?" the old man said.

Ihsan turned round and put his finger to his lips, signalling the old man that he should be quiet.

The man did not understand why he needed to be quiet, and looked at Ihsan in surprise. He asked: "Why do you want me to be quiet? I asked you a question. If you know the answer, just tell me. If you don't, then just shake your head. I cannot understand the kids in town. They are so strange," the old man grumbled.

When the person who was "it" saw the old man talking to someone behind the tree he realized that someone must be hiding there. He approached silently.

The old man – who was growing impatient – said:

"Obviously, no one has taught these children the following hadith:

"It is a charity to give directions to someone who is searching for a place."

مَنْ هَدَى زُقَاقًا كَانَ لَهُ مِثْلَ عِتْقِ رَقَبَةٍ

رواه الترمذي

He turned away and walked off. Ihsan felt ashamed of what he had done. He forgot about the game he was playing. He ran after the man and asked for his forgiveness. Then he took him to the place he was looking for.

SPOILSPORTS

A vni was a good boy most of the time. He just had one problem. He was very contentious and his friends didn't like his bad character. One day in the autumn the children were all sitting by the lake and talking about seas and lakes. They were saying that seas were deeper and colder than lakes.

As always, Avni took up the opposing view.

This time his friends didn't argue with him; they knew him very well by now.

They began to skip stones. Thin, flat stones skipped over the blue water like flying birds.

Faruk was able to skip his stones further than anyone else that day. His stones went a long way, skipping toward the horizon.

Avni felt jealous and said:

"Let me see your stones."

Faruk opened his hand and showed Avni his stones. His stones were no different than anyone else's. But spoilsport Avni always looked for a reason to pick a fight.

"Oh. You have taken the thinnest stones. Of course, such thin stones will go a long way, anyone can do that."

Faruk was an easy-going boy and said:

"All right; why don't we exchange stones? You take mine and I'll take yours."

But the result was the same.

Limping Haydar, who had been hurt in a traffic accident, approached Avni.

"You are in a bad mood today. And you're not very lucky either," he said to his friend, gently.

Avni was angry because he hadn't been able to skip the stones and shouted at Haydar,

"What do you know, you cripple!"

The other children became very angry with Avni. They all loved Haydar and hated to see anyone treat him badly. They told Avni that he had been very unfair and mean.

Avni's behavior goes against what our Prophet told us in the following hadith:

"Do not argue with your Muslim brothers and sisters! Do not make fun of them!"

لاَ تُمَارِ أَخَاكَ وَلاَ تُمَازِحْهُ

رواه الترمذي

THE CHERRY TREE

*A*li and Aisha climbed the cherry tree and began to eat all the ripe cherries.

Ali noticed that the cherries hanging at the branch-tips looked better.

"Those branches look thin and won't hold your weight. These are just as good," Aisha said to Ali to stop him from going to the thin branches.

But Ali didn't listen. He could think of nothing but those cherries. He crawled toward the

thin outer branches of the tree. Before long, he found himself on the ground along with a broken branch. He had broken not only the long branch of the tree; but also his leg. He had to stay home for many weeks; he could only watch the other children climbing the tree and picking all the cherries.

Ali's behavior was very greedy, wasn't it?

What a thought-provoking warning the following saying of our Prophet is:

"If a man had two streams full of gold, he would still ask for a third. Only the grave can satisfy man's greed."

لَوْ كَانَ لِابْنِ آدَمَ وَادِيَانِ مِنْ ذَهَبٍ لَأَحَبَّ

أَنْ يَكُونَ لَهُ ثَالِثٌ وَلاَ يَملَأُ فَاهُ إِلاَّ التُّرَابُ

رواه الترمذي.

THE BRAVE SON

*I*n ancient days, bandits would wait on the side of the road to rob and kidnap people, then they would sell them in the slave markets.

One day, a poor, old man was captured by the bandits. The leader of the bandits told the old man:

"If you don't want us to sell you in the slave market, you must bring us a hundred pieces of gold; only then we will let you go."

The old man wrote a letter to his family, saying:

"I know that you don't have enough money to buy my freedom. I am only writing this letter to let you know what happened to me."

The old man had a kind-hearted and brave son. When he got his father's letter he went to the bandits and said:

"Oh, my lords, I know that you will not release my father without a ransom. I am not asking you to do this. But you can see that he is a poor, weak, old man. If you sell him, you will not get a high price. Take me, and sell me, instead. You will get much more money this way."

The bandits liked this offer. But they said that they needed to ask their leader first. Their leader couldn't believe what he heard. He looked at the brave son in admiration and said:

"So there are still such brave sons living on earth. How wonderful! I would sacrifice myself to have such a brave person. Come, I give you your father's life for your sake. You and your father are both free to go!"

The old man and his brave son returned home, ecstatic at the outcome of their mishap.

This story reminds us of the following hadith of the Prophet:

"A child can never repay the rights he owes his father. Only if he finds his father as a slave and ransoms his freedom has he repaid his father's right in full."

لا يَجْزِي وَلَدٌ وَالِدًا إلاَّ

أَنْ يَجِدَهُ مَمْلُوكًا فَيَشْتَرِيَهُ فَيُعْتِقَهُ

رواه مسلم

THE KID

Necip loved goats very much; especially the little kids. His father gave him a kid as a gift to look after. Necip fed it and raised it during the summer. He loved it when the kid ran up to him and gently butted his hands.

Necip's father always told him:

"Don't leave the door open, otherwise the kid will come into the house and damage the furniture."

One day, Necip ran into the house to get his ball. He remembered what his father had told him, but didn't bother to close the door as he was going to be very quick. He didn't notice that the kid had run after him into the house.

While the kid was searching for Necip, it found itself in front of the big mirror in the living room. Another kid was looking at it. When the kid moved closer, the one in the mirror came closer, too. It went crazy when it saw the other kid approaching. The kid put its head down, ran at the mirror, and butted it. It wanted to teach the other goat a lesson. A huge crash was heard through the house. The mirror had been smashed into a hundred pieces.

If Necip had known what our Prophet had told his two young companions, Ibn Umar and Abdullah Ibn Amr he would never have ignored his father's advice:

"Obey your father!"

أَطِعْ أَبَاكَ

رواه أحمد

THE TALENTED CHILD

*T*hree women were returning from the market with baskets in their hands. They sat on a bench in order to take a break. They started to talk about their children.

The first woman mentioned how active her son was and said that he could walk on his hands for several minutes.

The second woman said her son could sing very well and that everyone loved his singing.

The third woman only listened. The other women asked her why she hadn't said anything. "My son has no special talent I can boast of," she said.

An old man who was passing by overheard their conversation and decided to follow them. When the women came to the street on which they lived they stopped again to rest, leaving their baskets on the ground. Their children saw them and came running to their mothers.

The first woman's son was turning cartwheels.

The second woman's son started to sing one of his mother's favorite songs. All the women applauded him.

The third woman's son came and asked: "Shall I help you, Mom?" and picked up the basket.

The women stopped the old man and asked him what he thought of their talented children.

"I saw only one talented boy," he said. "He is the one that is running to help his mother to carry her basket. He has behaved in accordance with the following hadith of our Prophet:

"I advise everyone to serve their mother."

أُوصِي امْرَأً بِأُمِّهِ

رواه ابن ماجه

THE PLASTIC PLATE

*T*here was a poor carpenter who was getting old. He had lost all his strength and now he was gradually losing his eyesight too. Because of his shaking hands he could no longer hold a spoon properly. He spilled more food on the tablecloth than he was able to put in his mouth.

His son and daughter-in-law were always telling him to be careful. They would get very angry with him, especially when the food dribbled down his chin. Finally they set a separate table away from theirs.

His little grandson Hasan felt very sad about his grandfather. He tried to help him by holding the spoon for him, so he would not spill his food.

One day, the old man accidentally dropped and broke his plate while he was eating. He looked at his children sitting at the table with tears in his eyes. They got very angry. They scolded him and broke his heart. From that time on they served him his meals in plastic plates.

One day, the carpenter's son told his wife not to put the fruit on the plastic plate, and told her to throw the plates into the trash.

Hasan took two of the plates and told his mother not to throw them away for they will need the plates in the future.

"What do you want them for?" his father asked.

Hasan replied:

"I will use them for your meals when you get older."

Hasan's parents felt very ashamed. They started to let their father eat with them once again.

If the son and his wife had only known that the best way to get into Heaven was to treat our parents well they would probably not have acted in such a way.

Our Prophet made this clear in the following Hadith:

"Allah's pleasure is gained in pleasing parents, and Allah's wrath is incurred in upsetting the parents."

رِضَى الرَّبِّ فِي رِضَى الْوَالِدِ

وَسَخَطُ الرَّبِّ فِي سَخَطِ الْوَالِدِ

رواه الترمذي

THE FOUNTAIN-PEN

Jelal was the son of a poor carpenter. He was sitting on the street corner and crying because he had lost his fountain-pen.

A well-dressed man was passing by. He stopped and asked Jelal what the matter was. When he heard his problem, he took a pen from his pocket and asked:

"Is this the pen you lost?"

Jelal tried to stop crying and answer:

"No, it is not. My pen was not as nice as that one."

The man admired Jelal's honesty.

"Because you are an honest boy and telling the truth, as a reward I am giving you this pen. Please accept it."

Our Prophet told us how God will reward honest people in the following hadith:

"Telling the truth leads to virtue and virtue leads to paradise."

إِنَّ الصِّدْقَ يَهْدِي إِلَى الْبِرِّ

وَإِنَّ الْبِرَّ يَهْدِي إِلَى الْجَنَّةِ

رواه البخاري

A LIAR

One day a man and a woman were on trial in a court. The judge came in and the session started. The woman made the first speech.

She pointed at the skinny man standing next to her and said: "This man attacked me and took away my honor," and she began to wail.

The man defended himself, saying: "She is lying, sir! This woman came to me while I was counting the money I had earned from selling my sheep. She wanted my money. She threatened me, saying that if I did not give it to her she would create problems for me. When I refused she started to scream."

After hearing them, the judge knew who was telling the truth and who was lying. But he said nothing.

Then he turned to the man and said angrily: "You attacked this poor woman and then come and tell us a pack of lies. Give all the money in your pocket to this woman or I will put you in jail."

Everybody was shocked. They hadn't expected the judge to react in such a way.

The woman gladly took the man's money and left the courtroom praying for the judge. As soon as she left, the judge told the man to go and follow her in order to get his money back. The man was once again shocked and rushed out quickly, hoping to get his money back.

A few minutes later, they were brought back into the courtroom again. The man was hurt, and had bruises and cuts on his face.

The woman spoke first again. She was very angry.

"Sir, this brute tried to take away the money you had given me."

The judge asked her:

"Did he manage to get it?"

"Do you think I would give up anything to this man?" the woman answered scornfully.

The judge turned and shouted at her:

"You shameless liar! You acted like an honest woman, claiming this man had attacked you. If that was true you would have fought harder to protect yourself than to protect the money which wasn't yours. Now give him back his money immediately!"

Before giving her a sentence, the judge reminded the woman of our Prophet's following hadith:

"Lying is immoral and immorality leads to hell."

إِيَّاكُمْ وَ الْكَذِبَ فَإِنَّ الْكَذِبَ يَهْدِي إِلَي الْفُجُورِ وَ إِنَّ الْفُجُورَ يَهْدِي إِلَي النَّارِ

رواه مسلم

THE CHESTNUT TREE

*H*usnu was talking to the judge, pointing to the suspect. "Sir! I left a diamond ring with this man before going abroad last year. Now I want my ring back, but he refuses to give it to me."

The judge asked Mistik Kahya, who was sitting in the box:

"Why didn't you give him his ring back?"

"He is lying. He didn't give me a ring," Kahya answered.

The judge turned to Husnu:

"Do you have a witness who saw you give this man the ring?"

"No, there was no one with us when I gave the ring to him under a chestnut tree."

The judge ordered Husnu to go and fetch him a branch from the chestnut tree.

A few minutes later the judge turned to Mistik Kahya and said:

"Where could he be? I wonder when he will come back. Go look out the window and tell me if he is coming."

Mistik Kahya did not even move from his place, but answered:

"He can't be back in less than three hours; it's a long way from here."

The judge turned to Mistik Kahya and said:

"Not only are you a liar, you are a fool as well! If you had not taken the ring you would not know where the chestnut tree was. Have you never heard the hadith of our Prophet?

"O people! Never lie! For lying and faith never come together."

يَا أَيُّهَا النَّاس إِيَّاكُمْ وَ الْكَذِبَ فَإِنَّ الْكَذِبَ

مُجَانِبٌ لِلْإِيمَانِ

رواه أحمد

The judge gave him a heavy punishment for his crime.

THE ECHO

L ittle Remzi was taking food to his father who was working in the fields. He spotted a shadowy figure behind the rocks at the top of the hill. Thinking that it was another child he shouted to him, saying "Heeeey!" A voice came back, saying "Heeeey!" from the hill top.

Not realizing it was an echo, he thought that another child was up there, making fun of him.

"Just wait and see what happens if I come up!"

The voice answered:

"Just wait and see what happens if I come up!"

Remzi got really angry and shouted at the top of his voice:

"Come out and let me see you, you coward!"

When the same answer came back to him he started to run toward the cliff. Soon he was tired, but he couldn't see anyone there. He thought that the other child must be hiding somewhere else. He climbed up the rocks, shouting all the while. He thought about what he would do to that other child when he caught him. But that cowardly child didn't dare to come out.

After a long time, he remembered his father. He must be very hungry by now. When he got to his father he told his father everything that had happened. His father listened to him and reminded his son of a proverb:

"He who speaks whatever he wants hears whatever he doesn't want to hear."

If Remzi had known the following saying of the Prophet he would not have acted in such a way:

"Let the one who believes in God and the Last Day speak good or remain silent."

مَنْ كَانَ يُؤْمِنُ بِاللَّهِ

وَالْيَوْمِ الْآخِرِ فَلْيَقُلْ خَيْرًا أَوْ لِيَصْمُتْ

رواه البخاري

BREAD

It was a cold winter day. Hasan was returning home with bread he had bought from the bakery. Suddenly he noticed a poor, skinny dog, which was so thin that all its ribs could be counted. The dog was staring at the bread in Hasan's basket and whining.

Hasan was deeply moved by this pitiful sight. He said to himself "If I give one of my loaves to this poor dog, My mother will be very angry." Then deciding that it was worth to take the risk of his mother's wrath, he put the basket down and started to break the bread into small pieces for the dog.

A man who was coming back from the bakery heard what Hasan had said. He secretly put one of his own loaves into Hasan's basket.

When Hasan arrived home he was surprised to find out that he had just as much bread as he had bought from the bakery!

Of course, Hasan could have explained this if he knew the following hadith of the Prophet:

"Charity never lessens wealth."

مَا نَقَصَتْ صَدَقَةٌ مِنْ مَالٍ

رواه مسلم

THE MISER

*I*hsan had a stingy uncle. He lived meagerly. He neither spent any of his money, nor gave anything to anyboy else. For this reason, no one liked him.

This poor miser exchanged everything he owned with gold, because he wanted to see everything he owned before his eyes. He then buried all the gold in his garden.

Every day he took the gold out from the ground and counted it coin by coin; then he buried it again in the same place.

One day, he couldn't find the gold anymore. Somebody must have stolen it. He went crazy with anger.

Ihsan, when he learned about what had happened, went to visit his uncle and said:

"Don't cry for the money. It was not yours. It didn't belong to you. If it had, you wouldn't have buried it in the garden, but you would have used it for your benefit."

Our Prophet who took refuge in God from stinginess said in his hadith:

"A stingy person is far from Allah, far from paradise and far from other human beings."

الْبَخِيلُ بَعِيدٌ مِنْ اللَّهِ بَعِيدٌ

مِنْ الْجَنَّةِ بَعِيدٌ مِنْ النَّاسِ

رواه الترمذي

THE SHOES

*I*t was a long, hard winter. Sadi was very cold, because his shoes were worn and they let the water in. For the first time, he was sorry that his family was poor. He thought how nice it would be if they had enough money to buy a thick coat and some good shoes.

One day Sadi was returning from school with his bag in hand. He stopped before the central mosque just as the adhan for afternoon prayer was being called. Sadi liked to pray in the mosque, so he went into the courtyard and walked up to

the fountains to perform his ablution. He left his school bag on the bench and rolled up his sleeves.

He knew almost everybody who was performing ablution there.

He sat at a fountain and took off his shoes. His socks were dirty and wet. Angrily he threw one of his torn shoes on the ground. Then he saw a man prforming ablution next to him. This man washed one leg and then stood up. Sadi noticed that that the man had only one leg.

Now he was embarrassed. He had been worried about his shoes, but that man had only one leg. Maybe he had a lot of money to buy shoes; but money wasn't everything.

After completing his prayer, Sadi began to pray to God, raising his hands high. He thanked God for his strong legs.

How wonderful is the following saying of our Prophet:

"Always be content with less. Then you will be the best at thanking God."

وَكُنْ قَنِعًا تَكُنْ أَشْكَرَ النَّاسِ
رواه ابن ماجه

THE CAR

*H*ikmet was a good student. He was going to a secondary school far from his home. Everyday he went to school by bus and returned home the same way.

Hikmet had several hobbies. One of them was cars. On the way to school, he could tell his friends the model and make of every car they saw on the road. He was a little sad, as his family didn't have a car. However, he never complained about this to his family, because he knew that they couldn't afford one. His father was a civil servant and barely earned enough to feed their family of four. It would be silly to ask for a car. It would also be unfair to ask more from his father who was doing his best for his family.

Hikmet's friend Ahmad lived in the same neighborhood. But he never took the bus to school. He always walked the long way there and back. Hikmet couldn't understand why his friend did this.

One day, it was rainy and cold. Hikmet was waiting at the bus stop with his friends. Ahmad passed by in front of them, ignoring the rain.

"Ahmad, the bus will be here soon. Why are you walking?" Hikmet asked.

"Thank you but I have to stop by somewhere else first," he replied as he kept on walking.

The same event took place a few more times in the following days. Hikmet started to wonder why Ahmad was not taking the bus. One day, he told his mother about this.

Hikmet's mother knew Ahmad's family well. Ahmad's father had died a few years ago, leaving six children behind. His poor mother tried to earn money and feed his family by cleaning other people's houses. Ahmad couldn't take the bus simply because his family couldn't afford it.

Hikmet felt sad and ashamed. He had wished for a car, but there were thousands of people living in the same city who didn't have enough money for food or didn't have a proper house to sleep in. He thanked God for everything that he had.

If Hikmet had heard the following hadith of our Prophet he would never have felt sad about not having a car:

"You must compare yourself to those who are lower than you, not to those who are higher than you."

انْظُرُوا إِلَى مَنْ أَسْفَلَ مِنْكُمْ

وَلاَ تَنْظُرُوا إِلَى مَنْ هُوَ فَوْقَكُمْ

رواه مسلم

SMOKE

Once upon a time there was a man called Hatem. He was a rich and generous man. He had many herds of animals that grazed in the grassy fields, and he loved to share his wealth with others.

Hatem had a pitch-black horse called Smoke. Everybody admired this horse for its speed. It ran like a flying eagle. Hatem regarded Smoke as the apple of his eye, and he would not give it up for anything.

Finally, the fame of Hatem's wealth and his beautiful horse reached the ears of the Sultan. When the Sultan heard about him he called his Grand Vizier and said:

"I want to test Hatem's generosity. Ask him to give me Smoke. Let's see what he does."

The Sultan's men set off the next day. One night when it was raining very hard they reached Hatem's house and became his guests.

Hatem greeted them with joy and warmth. He ordered his servants to prepare food for his guests. Soon an excellent table was set for dinner and they all sat down to eat. After the meal the guests were put up in very comfortable beds, where they slept soundly.

The next morning when the guests explained why they had come, Hatem became very sad and didn't know what to do in his great sorrow.

"What a pity!" he said, "I wished you had told me what the Sultan wanted as soon as you had arrived. I know that you love horsemeat, and last night, as due to the bad weather I couldn't find anything else to offer you. So, I slaughtered Smoke last night for us to eat, as I had no other alternative."

But even Hatem's generosity paled next to our Prophet's, who once gave a single man a gift of a hundred camels!

Our glorious Prophet stated in the following hadith how great a character trait generosity was:

"A generous person is close to God, close to human beings, close to Paradise, and far from Hell."

السَّخِيُّ قَرِيبٌ مِنَ اللَّهِ قَرِيبٌ مِنَ الْجَنَّةِ

قَرِيبٌ مِنَ النَّاسِ بَعِيدٌ مِنَ النَّارِ

رواه الترمذي

SUN-DRIED BRICKS

Once upon a time, there was a poor man called "Murat the Genuine." He was a good-hearted man and a devout Muslim. One day he found a gold ingot in the shape of a sun-dried brick while he was repairing the walls of his house. He was so happy that he didn't know what to do.

He began to think: "Finally I am no longer poor. Now I will build a mansion for myself and furnish its rooms with the best furniture and lay the floors with alabaster. The garden will be full of flowers and all kinds of fruit trees where the most beautiful birds will sing."

That night he had lovely dreams.

The next day, he imagined how many servants he would have, the gardeners, cooks and butlers who would all work in his mansion.

The following day he continued to dream such lovely things. All day and all night he would just dream; he didn't even eat, drink, or pray to God and thank Him for the health and wealth he had been given!

One day when Murat was walking outside the town, dreaming his dreams, he saw a man cutting sun-dried bricks by the wall of the cemetery.

The man was digging out the soil and mixing it with water and straw, which he then put in a mold to make the bricks.

The man told Murat that the bricks made from the soil of the graveyard were sturdier than those made from other soil. Murat was shocked. He felt as if he had been punched. Suddenly he awoke from his dreams and, continuing on his way, scolded himself.

"Shame on you! Poor, absent-minded man! One day they will make bricks from the soil that covers you. You lost your way when you found that gold. You forgot to pray and thank God. However, life takes many things back each day. You are getting closer to death with every day that passes. Stop dreaming and indulging in fantasies! This is a gift from God; spend your money wisely, don't waste it and don't spend it foolishly!"

Just then, the adhan for noon-prayer rose up from the minarets.

When he heard this, Murat went towards the mosque with peace in his heart; he now knew what was right and good.

If Murat had known earlier the following hadith he wouldn't have undergone such a time of confusion:

"If I had gold as much as Mount Uhud, I would not want to keep it with me more than three days other than the amount of my debt."

لَوْ كَانَ لِي مِثْلُ أُحُدٍ ذَهَبًا مَا يَسُرُّنِي
أَنْ لَا يَمُرَّ عَلَيَّ ثَلَاثٌ وَعِنْدِي
مِنْهُ شَيْءٌ إِلَّا شَيْءٌ أُرْصِدُهُ لِدَيْنٍ
رواه البخاري.

THE GUEST

*H*amdi was playing in the garden when he saw a poor old man with a white beard in the street. The man was walking slowly. He stopped at the gate of Hamdi's house, a beautiful mansion, to take a breath.

"My son, do you mind if I spend the night in this guesthouse?" he said.

"This is not a guesthouse." Hamdi replied smiling.

"What is it then?"

"It is our home."

"Really? That's nice. Well...who built this mansion?"

"My grandfather!"

"Who inherited it after him?"

"My father!"

"So, who will inherit it after your father?"

"Probably me."

The old man smiled and looked at Hamdi's face for a little while. Then he said:

"As the owner of this house keeps changing, then it means you are all guests in this house, doesn't it?" Then he stood up and continued walking.

When school started that year, Hamdi told this story in his religion lesson. When some of the students thought that the old man had spoken nonsense, their teacher reminded them of the following hadith of the Prophet:

"My relation with this world is as a traveler who continues his journey after having rested under a tree."

مَا أَنَا فِي الدُّنْيَا إِلاَّ كَرَاكِبٍ اسْتَظَلَّ

تَحْتَ شَجَرَةٍ ثُمَّ رَاحَ وَتَرَكَهَا

رواه الترمذي

THE WOODSMAN

There once was a poor woodsman during the time of Prophet Moses (peace be upon him). He collected woods from the mountains, carried them on his back, and sold them at the market. He lived on the little income he earned from this work. The work was hard, but the woodsman never tired of it.

One of his neighbors was also doing the same work but he had a donkey to take the

wood to the market. This made the woodsman very jealous.

One day the poor woodsman went to Moses to explain his problem.

"I always have many sores on my back from carrying the wood. I have yet to live a peaceful day. Please, when you go before the Lord, explain my situation to Him and ask Him to grant me a donkey to take my wood to the market."

When Moses talked to Allah Almighty, he repeated what the woodsman had said.

Allah replied:

"This servant of mine is suffering from jealousy. Until he rids himself of this illness he won't feel comfortable. He must give it up. Nowadays the other woodsman's donkey is sick. Tell him to pray for his neighbor's donkey. If he does so and the donkey gets well then I will give him a donkey too."

When Moses reported this to the poor woodsman, he became even more jealous and said:

"No, I can't pray to God for the recovery of my neighbor's donkey. I am happy with what I have and I don't need a donkey from God. I hope He doesn't cure the donkey – that will be enough for me."

Jealousy is nothing but an illness. If some-one is suffering from this disease, he or she will never be happy. The reason why the woodsman was tired and was never at ease was because of his jealousy, not the wood he was carrying.

How wonderfully our beloved Prophet explains this situation in the following hadith!

"Don't be jealous. It destroys good deeds just as fire destroys wood."

إِيَّاكُمْ وَالْحَسَدَ فَإِنَّ الْحَسَدَ يَأْكُلُ الْحَسَنَاتِ كَمَا تَأْكُلُ النَّارُ الْحَطَبَ

رواه أبو داود

THE BLOODY FILE

O ne Day Adam was going shopping. He got up early in the morning and went to the market. One by one, he placed all the items he was buying in his small shopping bag. He had no idea that the file he had bought from the hardware store would pierce the bag of liver he bought from the butcher's.

When Adam came home from shopping, he took out the bloody file and left it by the door to clean it up later. A few minutes later, he noticed that a hungry cat had been attracted by the smell of liver and was licking the file with its tongue.

The strange thing is that the blood on the file was increasing instead of decreasing.

Adam felt sorry for the poor cat, but he chased it away to protect it from hurting itself.

The cat went a little away and frowned at Adam. It was hungry and needed some food, and why was this brutal man chasing him away?

What the poor cat didn't realize was that the blood it had tasted was his own. It had cut its own tongue with the sharp file. When Adam told his father what had happened he laughed and said:

"Some people are like your kitty. They don't realize that the wrong things they do will hurt them one someday. They get upset when people try to stop them from hurting themselves, just like that cat."

Adam grumbled: "We should just let them do the wrong and get their lesson by themselves."

His father heard him and replied:

"Leaving them with their wrong actions is a shortcoming on our part. Our duty is to try to deter people from doing wrong. In this way we not only help those people, but society as well."

Then he recited the following hadith to Adam:

"When any of you sees something disapproved (by God), change it with your hand. If you cannot do this, then change it with your tongue.

If you cannot do this, then change it with your heart."

مَنْ رَأَى مِنْكُمْ مُنْكَرًا فَلْيُغَيِّرْهُ بِيَدِه

فَإِنْ لَمْ يَسْتَطِعْ فَبِلِسَانِهِ فَإِنْ لَمْ يَسْتَطِعْ فَبِقَلْبِهِ

رواه مسلم

THE DOG

It was harvest time and Memis and his wife were harvesting their field. As they worked, their little baby slept under a tree, watched over by their dog Karabas.

A little while later Memis and his wife took a break. When they went up where their baby was sleeping, they witnessed a terrible scene. Their baby was lying face down in the cradle, motionless, while Karabas was lying a few yards away, covered in blood.

Memis went mad. He thought Karabas had killed his baby so he struck the dog with his scythe. Poor Karabas died instantly.

Memis was even more shocked when his wife told him their baby was fine, just sleeping. They didn't know what to think until they caught sight of a huge snake lying dead a few feet away. They realized that Karabas got wounded after fighting the big snake and had sacrificed his life saving their baby. They felt extremely sorry about the big mistake they had made.

If Memis had acted in accordance with what the Prophet had ordered in the following hadith they would have been happier:

"Acting with caution is from Allah, and haste is from the Devil."

الأَنَاةُ مِنْ اللهِ وَالْعَجَلَةُ مِنْ الشَّيْطَانِ

رواه الترمذي

THE YELLOW COW

Aunt Aisha planted beans in her garden. The beans sprouted in a very short time as the weather had been good.

One day Aunt Aisha woke up to the loud bellows of a cow in the garden. She rushed out to see what was happening. Her neighbor's yellow cow had broken into her garden and it was trampling the young beans.

Aunt Aisha was petrified when she saw all her efforts going to waste. The yellow cow with a rope still around her neck kept bellowing outside her stable. Aunt Aisha, who was getting angrier every second, walked towards the cow with a big stick in her hand.

Just then, her neighbor's wife came by running. She started to talk with a sad voice:

"Her poor calf died yesterday. She broke her ropes three times this morning. She is running around, looking for her calf."

When Aunt Aisha heard this, the stick fell from her hand. She began to pat the grieving cow, looking into her sorrowful eyes.

"I see .... She is missing her baby," she said.

She totally forgot about the beans.

Aunt Aisha performed a simple act of kindness.

How commendable Aunt Aisha's change of behavior was, was it not? It was just as our Prophet ordered in the following Hadith:

"Be afraid of God and do not be cruel against dumb animals."

اتَّقُوا اللَّهَ فِي هَذِهِ الْبَهَائِمِ الْمُعْجَمَةِ

رواه أبو داود

SOURCES OF THE AHADITH

The Birds: Nasaī, *Kitāb al-Imāmah*, Hadith no. 48.

A Thorn: Tirmizi, *Kitāb al-Birr*, Hadith no. 16.

The Coat: Bukhārī, *Kitāb al-Sawm*, Hadith no. 56.

The Mirror: Abū Dāvūd, *Kitāb al-Adab*, Hadith no. 49.

The 'Meanie': Bukhārī, *Kitāb al-Mazālim*, Hadith no. 3.

A Ghost: Muslim, *Kitāb al-Adhkār*, Hadith no. 38.

A Neighbor in Paradise: Muslim, *Kitāb al-Adhkār*, Hadith no. 38.

Tooth Medicine: Muslim, *Kitāb al-Imān*, Hadith no. 164.

The Wallet: Tirmizī, *Kitāb al-Birr*, Hadith no. 35.

The Poison: Tirmizī, *Kitāb al-Birr*, Hadith no. 27.

The Belt: Tirmizī, *Kitāb al-Birr*, Hadith no. 58.

Anger: Bukhārī, *Kitāb al-Adab*, Hadith no. 76.

The Race: Muslim, *Kitāb al-Jannah*, Hadith no. 64.

The Gold: Muslim, *Kitāb al-Imān*, Hadith no. 147.

The Thief: Bukhārī, *Kitāb al-hudūd*, Hadith no. 7.

The Morsel: Ibn Abī Shaibah, *Al-Musannaf (Hūt) Vol. 6*, Hadith no. 164.

The Money: Muslim, *Kitāb al-Birr*, Hadith no. 5.

The Mediator: Tirmizī, *Kitāb al-'Ilm*, Hadith no. 14.

Hide and Seek: Tirmizī, *Kitāb al-Birr*, Hadith no. 37.

Spoilsports: Tirmizī, *Kitāb al-Birr*, Hadith no. 58.

The Cherry Tree: Tirmizī, *Kitāb al-Zuhd*, Hadith no. 27.

The Brave Son: Muslim, *Kitāb al-'Itq*, Hadith no. 25.

The Kid: Ahmad b. Hanbal, *Musnad vol. II*, Hadith no. 20, 164, 206.

The Talented Child: Ibn Majah, *Kitāb al-Adab*, Hadith no. 1.

The Plastic Plate: Tirmizī, *Kitāb al-Birr*, Hadith no. 3

The Fountain-Pen: Bukhārī, *Kitāb al-Adab*, Hadith no. 69.

A Liar: Muslim, *Kitāb al-Birr*, Hadith no. 103.

The Chestnut Tree: Ahmad b. Hanbal, *Musnad vol. I*, Hadith no. 5.

The Echo: Bukhārī, *Kitāb al-Adab*, Hadith no. 31.

Bread: Muslim, *Kitāb al-Birr*, Hadith no. 69

The Miser: Tirmizī, *Kitāb al-Birr*, Hadith no. 40.

The Shoes: Ibn Majah, *Kitāb al-Zuhd*, Hadith no. 24

The Car: Muslim, *Kitāb al-Adab*, Hadith no. 8.

Smoke: Tirmizī, *Kitāb al-Birr*, Hadith no. 40.

Sun-Dried Bricks: Bukhārī, *Kitāb al-Istiqrāz*, Hadith no. 3.

The Guest: Tirmizī, *Kitāb al-Zuhd*, Hadith no. 44

The Woodsman: Abū Dāvūd, *Kitāb al-Adab*, Hadith no. 44.

The Bloody File: Muslim, *Kitāb al-Imān*, Hadith no. 49.

The Dog: Tirmizī, *Kitāb al-Birr*, Hadith no. 66

The Yellow Cow: Abū Dāvūd, *Kitāb al-Jihād*, Hadith no. 44.

Printed in India